The purpose of this study guide is to provide supplemental educational material. It is not intended as a substitute or replacement of WHY ARE ALL THE BLACK KIDS SITTING TOGETHER IN THE CAFETERIA?.

Published by SuperSummary, www.supersummary.com

ISBN – 9798671001006

For more information or to learn about our complete library of study guides, please visit http://www.supersummary.com

Please submit any comments, corrections, or questions to:
http://www.supersummary.com/support/

TABLE OF CONTENTS

First published in 1997, *Why Are All the Black Kids Sitting Together in the Cafeteria?: And Other Conversations About Race* addresses race and racism in the United States from a psychologist's perspective. Beverly Daniel Tatum is a clinical psychologist with extensive experience in researching racial identity development. We need to learn how to have productive dialogues about race and racism, and to do that we need to understand how our racial identities form and how they affect our lives.

This guide is based on the updated edition released in 2017, which includes updates to the text as well as a new Prologue and Epilogue covering developments over the 20 years since the book was originally published. This guide also mirrors many of Tatum's choices with regard to language, including the capitalization of all racial and ethnic terms (including "White" and "Black"), the preference for the gender-neutral term "Latinx" over "Latino" or "Latina," and the variable use of terms referring to the same group (e.g. "Native American," "Native people," and "American Indian").

The Prologue surveys how racism continues to be a pervasive problem in the United States. People of color are targeted by police brutality, mass incarceration, voter suppression, segregation, microaggressions, hate crimes, and other injustices. After defining racism and introducing the basics of identity development in Part 1, Tatum explores the process of racial identity development for Black Americans throughout their childhood, adolescence, and adulthood in Part 2. Their encounters with racism lead to an exploration of what it means to be Black. They are surrounded by cultural images and messages that devalue Blackness, but the process of finding a positive racial identity can be aided by having the support of same-race peers.

Many White Americans don't think much about their own racial group, which is the definition of White privilege. They may see themselves as racially tolerant or even "color-blind" but fail to recognize the existence of pervasive racial inequalities. If they do begin to notice racism, however, this may trigger an exploration of what it means to be White, which begins the process of active participation in an anti-racist society. In Part 3, Tatum describes how this process often leads to feelings of guilt and isolation, but that White people can also attain a positive racial identity rooted in antiracism. Part 4 surveys some of the experiences of other people of color. Latinxs may struggle with the devaluation of their Spanish language, Native people may struggle with the demeaning caricatures of their group, Asian Pacific Americans may struggle with being stereotyped as the "model minority" who don't experience racism, and people of Middle Eastern and North African heritage may struggle with Islamophobia and being stereotyped as "terrorists." Multiracial individuals may find identities imposed upon them based on their appearance, while children of color in White families may grow up feeling like perpetual outsiders. All of these groups consist of people with an incredibly wide range of backgrounds and experiences, but they are all affected by racism.

In the final section of the book, Tatum emphasizes the importance of breaking silence regarding racism. By providing readers with an understanding of racial identity development, Tatum hopes that educators will have a better understanding of how to teach in their racially mixed classrooms, parents will have a better understanding of how to talk with their children about race and racism, and everyone will have a better understanding of their own daily lives and interactions. We need to be able to talk about racism in order to change it. This book is intended to help readers have the dialogues that are needed to bring about that change.

CHAPTER SUMMARIES AND ANALYSES

Prologue-Introduction

Prologue Summary: "'Why Are All the Black Kids *Still* Sitting Together in the Cafeteria' and Other Conversations About Race in the Twenty-First Century"

The 20th anniversary edition begins with a lengthy Prologue which surveys how race relations have changed (or not changed) since the book was first published in 1997. Despite growing racial and ethnic diversity in the American population, segregation persists. The legacy of discriminatory policies and practices in the real estate industry means that residential segregation remains a pervasive issue in the present day. Meanwhile, courts have curtailed school desegregation strategies, meaning that students have returned to attending schools based on where they live. Public schools today are more segregated than they were in 1980.

Beyond the persistence of segregation, there have been several setbacks in the past 20 years. There has been a backlash against affirmative action programs, which has caused the enrolment of Black, Latinx, and American Indian students to plummet at universities. The Great Recession of 2008 has had a disproportionate impact on Black and Latinx families, causing them to lose their homes and jobs at a higher rate than Whites. Families of color have also been torn apart by mass incarceration. Ever since Ronald Reagan declared a "War on Drugs" in the 1980s, Black and Latino men have made up about 90 percent of those imprisoned for drug offenses in many states—despite the majority of illegal drug users and dealers being White. Most of these incarcerated people have no history of violence and have not played a significant role in the drug trade, but harsh mandatory sentences have increased the length of time they spend in prison.

If there is one event in the past 20 years that has been a sign of positive change, it is the election of Barack Obama in 2008, "the first African American man to overcome the most symbolic of racial barriers" (17). While his victory was a sign of hope for many people, it generated anxiety and even fear for some White people. It seemed to them as though the racial hierarchy was being threatened and society was changing in unpredictable ways. Although voter fraud occurs very rarely, many state governments have since passed laws making it more difficult to vote, which usually impacts the poor and people of color the most. There has also been a substantial rise in hate group membership and hate crimes, and it is not just older generations who take part. There is the myth that we are now living in a postracial society in which racial issues have become a thing of the past, but Tatum argues that we have become more "color-silent" than "color-blind." We avoid talking about race, but we still see racial categories and we still have implicit biases.

Those implicit biases can manifest themselves in police encounters—including who gets shot and who doesn't, or who is given the benefit of the doubt and who isn't. In 2012, the police accepted George Zimmerman's account after he killed Trayvon Martin—a Black teenager who was unarmed—and claimed it was self-defense. Zimmerman was arrested after the incident became a national news story, but he was found not guilty. Martin's death gave rise to the Black Lives Matter movement, which was further amplified over the following years after Eric Garner was strangled to death, John Crawford III was shot and killed while shopping at a Walmart, and Michael Brown was shot and killed in the streets of Ferguson, Missouri.

Brown's death sparked outrage in Ferguson, where the police have long discriminated against Black residents. A new generation of young activists were furious that the police could shoot Black people in the streets and face no repercussions. Black Lives Matter stood out from older generations of activists in that women and queer people have played a central role in the movement. The fall of 2015 saw another surge of activism, this time on college campuses across the US and Canada. The most prominent protests occurred at the University of Missouri, where students were angered that the school administration was failing to address incidents of bigotry aimed at Black students. After several weeks of protests, the university's president resigned.

Discussions of race and racism in the US tend to focus heavily on Black-White relations, and this often means that the experiences of other people of color are brushed aside. Native communities also suffer from police violence (and are killed by police at an even higher rate than Black people) and incarceration disparities. All marginalized groups risk experiencing microaggressions in their daily lives, which are the everyday slights and insults a person might receive due to their race, religion, sexual orientation, or other aspect of their identity. People of Asian ancestry are routinely asked where they are from or told to "go back home," leading to a "persistent sense of otherness" (52) according to one Chinese American journalist. These microaggressions can take a toll on a person psychologically and even result in physical health problems.

The lead-up to the 2016 presidential election heightened concerns for people of color. Donald Trump's speeches were marked by anti-Mexican and anti-Muslim rhetoric, and at various points during his campaign he also insulted Black people, women, and people with disabilities. He was endorsed by White nationalists and seemed to covertly encourage their support. In the aftermath of multiple deadly shootings, Trump responded with a speech emphasizing law and order, while his Democratic rival Hillary Clinton called for healing and unity. In the end, most White voters chose Trump, which one commentator called a "White-lash against a changing country" (64). Most voters of color did not choose Trump, but it is also important to ask who was not able to vote at all. The 2016 election was the first to be held after fourteen states had enacted new voting restrictions.

In the days following Trump's electoral win, there was a sharp rise in hate-motivated incidents, including hateful graffiti, harassment, and occasionally violence. One Asian American woman reported that discrimination had become more "public and unashamed" (67) under Trump's presidency. Through their words, leaders are able to strongly influence public sentiment. If they utilize "us versus them" rhetoric which shows hostility toward others, then people feel a greater sense of threat. If they use more inclusionary rhetoric, then the sense of threat is reduced. While many people would assume that race relations have surely improved over time, Tatum highlights that the past 20 years have given us countless Black people who have died at the hands of the police, a Black president who could do little about it, and a White president who has ushered in a new era of heightened bigotry and hate.

Introduction Summary: "A Psychologist's Perspective"

In a brief introductory chapter, Tatum addresses what she, as a psychologist, can contribute to public discourse about race and racism. She aims to provide readers with an understanding of racial identity development, which can aid them in understanding what is happening in their own cross-racial interactions and how racism operates in their own lives. Tatum hopes that these insights will equip readers with the tools they need to have productive dialogues about race and racism—that instead of being too intimidated to talk about racial issues, people can have the conversations that are necessary to face racism and change it.

Both in her lectures as well as in this book, Tatum draws heavily on conversations she has had in her own life. Because she is a Black woman who has lived and worked in predominantly White settings, this means that there is a particular focus on Black-White relations. Nevertheless, she aims to represent the experiences of Latinx, Asian American, Native, Middle Eastern, and biracial people in this book as well.

Prologue-Introduction Analysis

The Prologue focuses overwhelmingly on how people of color have continued to be oppressed in the US over the past 20 years. There tends to be the assumption that society progresses over time. Obama's election in particular was a highly symbolic moment for the country, in which it seemed to many people that "race [was] no longer a barrier to opportunity for people of color" (23). Yet Tatum's review of racial issues over the past few decades shows how there has been stagnation—or even regression—in many regards. She counteracts the narrative that racism is dead by showing all the ways that it continues to operate in American society. Segregation still exists, as do incarceration disparities and voter suppression strategies. People of color are disproportionately victims of police violence, they are economically disadvantaged, and they have increasingly been targets of microaggressions and hate crimes since the 2016 election. It is tempting to believe that things are better than they were in 1997, but Tatum provides a long list of evidence to the contrary.

Much of the Prologue highlights the importance of leadership, and especially the leadership provided by US presidents. Their importance is not just due to their power to influence US laws and policies, but also their power to influence public discourse. Obama's presidency inspired mixed reactions among the American population—many felt hopeful when they saw a Black man could reach the highest office in the country, many felt that hope wane when they saw that racism was still very much a reality despite Obama's achievements and power, and some White people felt threatened and feared that the racial hierarchy of the country was being thrown into question. The "us versus them" rhetoric of the 2016 election and Trump's presidency have heightened that sense of threat, leading to more vocal and blatant hatred aimed at people of color and other marginalized groups. Although both Obama and Trump are highly influential figures, Tatum portrays Trump as far more effective in entrenching racism than Obama was in fighting it. It is easier to reinforce the status quo than it is to change it.

Discussions of racial issues in the US are quite often framed in terms of Black-White relations, and Tatum acknowledges in the Introduction that this is largely true of this book as well. Because this book draws heavily on conversations she has had in her own professional and personal life, this is perhaps an inevitable outcome. When discussing other racial groups in the Prologue, she often utilizes outside sources. Tatum herself may not have any personal experience living as a Native person or as an Asian American, but members of these groups still have a voice in the book through the extensive use of quotations.

Given the long list of setbacks and injustices described in the Prologue, Tatum recognizes that it will probably not inspire much hope in readers. Nevertheless, she herself has hope for the future. As she explains in the Introduction, she believes in the importance of dialogue in producing social change. Insofar as this book is successful in achieving Tatum's goal of helping readers to understand and talk about racial issues, then this book can be a part of that change.

Part 1

Part 1: "A Definition of Terms"

Chapter 1 Summary: "Defining Racism"

From early childhood, we receive distorted and incomplete information about people who are different from us. We learn stereotypes from images in the media, we hear ethnic jokes from our family and friends, and at school we don't learn as much about the accomplishments of people of color. This misinformation lays the foundation for prejudice, or the preconceived notions we have about other people. Living in a racist society is like living in a smoggy city—we all inevitably breathe the smog in. That is to say, we are all inevitably prejudiced. Although it is not our fault that we are prejudiced, we are responsible for doing something about it. By examining our own prejudices, reflecting carefully on what we say and do, and educating ourselves about marginalized groups of people, we can ensure that our children don't inherit our polluted air.

In Tatum's view, racism is not merely the expression of prejudice, but a "system of advantage based on race" (87). There are systematic advantages for White people in the United States, and systematic disadvantages for people of color. White privilege means being able to apply for jobs and housing without having to worry about experiencing racial discrimination. White people can speak or act however they please without it being labelled as a "White" behavior or viewpoint. Whether they are aware of it or not, racism gives White people a number of advantages in life, and that idea often causes them discomfort. It is far more comfortable to believe that racism is simply about individual prejudice, but acknowledging the existence of systemic racism is necessary to stop it from being perpetuated.

Tatum clarifies that viewing racism in this way does not mean that all Whites are bad people, nor does it mean that people of color are never bigoted. But it does mean that, in a White-dominated society, White people are the only ones who systematically benefit from racism. Overtly racist behavior—such as the image of a cross-burning Ku Klux Klan member—is known as active racism. Passive racism is less obvious, but takes place when someone laughs at a racist joke, or when someone accepts the exclusion of people of color from school curricula. Both of them serve to perpetuate the cycle of racism, which Tatum compares this to the moving walkways at an airport. The active racist is walking quickly down the walkway while the passive racist is standing still, but the conveyor belt moves them both to the same destination. It is only by being actively antiracist—by turning around and walking quickly in the opposite direction on the conveyor belt—that the cycle of racism can be interrupted. Racism is not "a thing of the past" (83), as one of Tatum's students believed. It remains very much present, and it is harmful for both people of color as well as White people.

Chapter 2 Summary: "The Complexity of Identity"

Our identities are shaped by social, cultural, and historical factors. Identity formation is a process that begins in adolescence and continues throughout the rest of a person's life. To a large extent, how we view ourselves is dependent on how others see us—they are "the mirror in which we see ourselves" (99). Tatum has carried out a classroom exercise in which she asks her students to make a list of descriptors about themselves. Many of her students of color identify as their race or ethnicity, while her White students rarely bring up being White. Her female students often identify as female, but her male students rarely mention their gender. The same pattern applies when it comes to religion and sexual orientation. When a person is a member of a dominant social group, that facet of their identity is taken for granted because it is what the dominant culture views to be normal.

The elements of our identity that are more salient to us are those that other people view as abnormal. As a child, Tatum was the only Black student in her class. She became aware as she grew up that her race marked her as an "other." People can also be "others" on the basis of gender, sexual orientation, socioeconomic status, and other dimensions, and each of these has a corresponding form of oppression—sexism, heterosexism, classism, and so forth. Many of us are simultaneously members of dominant and targeted groups, but it is the latter that we tend to focus on. Although this book focuses on race and racism, Tatum recommends that readers try to draw on their own experiences of being in dominant and subordinate groups. A White person with a disability may not understand easily what it is like to be targeted by racism, but they could think about their experiences with ableism. An able-bodied Black person could similarly reflect on the advantages they overlook.

Dominant groups hold more power in society. While subordinate groups are virtually forced to learn about and adapt to the dominant culture, the dominant group is often ignorant about the experiences of the subordinates. The dominant group is seen as the norm and they have a ubiquitous presence in movies, books, and newspapers. The subordinate group, on the other hand, is often labeled inferior and they tend to be represented in the media as mere stereotypes. Members of the subordinate group may not respond to oppression as a way to protect themselves. Some may reject the world of the dominant group and refuse to adapt to it, and some may internalize the images and messages which portray the dominant group as superior to the subordinate group, potentially leading to self-hate. No matter what strategies they may use, living in an oppressive system takes its toll.

Part 1 Analysis

Tatum's definition of racism goes against what many White people have spent their lives believing. When they think of racism, they tend to think of people who are overtly bigoted—people who commit hate crimes, who use racial slurs, or who believe that Whites are genetically superior. Many White people look down on such behaviors, and they may become angry when stories of bigotry make the news. Meanwhile, the subtler, more pervasive systemic racism continues to operate without them taking as much notice. This means they have a hard time seeing how they are privileged due to their race, and they have a hard time accepting it because it goes against the narrative that the US is a meritocracy in which everyone has equal opportunities in life. The idea that they have spent their lives being complicit in oppression is a profoundly uncomfortable one.

There are most likely some readers who will be reluctant to accept that they benefit from racism, and there are likewise some who are probably skeptical of Tatum's claim that everyone is prejudiced. These claims can easily feel like personal attacks. Tatum is therefore careful to clarify that not all White people are hateful bigots, nor is it our fault that we all have prejudices. The important thing is what we do about it going forward. Her goal is not to assign blame, but to encourage readers to reflect more carefully on their own beliefs, assumptions, words, and actions. As uncomfortable as these truths may be, confronting them is a necessary step to interrupting racism.

Tatum uses several analogies in these chapters to illustrate how prejudice and racism function in society. She compares prejudice to a "smog" that saturates the air to show how all members of society have inevitably acquired prejudices. We may not want to believe that we have breathed it in, but it is unavoidable when it is all around us. To show how active and passive racism both lead to the preservation of the current social order, Tatum gives the example of two people on a moving walkway. One is walking and the other standing still, but the end result is the same.

She also draws on a number of anecdotes from her classroom and her own experiences. Instead of just stating that some White people are oblivious to the continued presence of racism, she illustrates it with a story about a

White student who believed that it didn't exist anymore. Instead of just claiming that people identify more strongly with the subordinate groups they are a member of, she demonstrates it through the classroom activity she has done with her students. By telling these stories, Tatum grounds her arguments in evidence from her everyday interactions and experiences.

Part 2

Part 2: "Understanding Blackness in a White Context"

Chapter 3 Summary: "The Early Years"

When they are as young as 3 years old, children begin to notice differences in physical appearance, especially skin color. When Tatum's oldest son, Jonathan, was in preschool, a White classmate asked him if his skin was brown because he drank too much chocolate milk. The classmate had already begun to see Whiteness as the norm. His question was not a sign of prejudice, but confusion. Tatum also tells the story of a 5-year-old Black boy who wished he was White because he wanted to become a paramedic, like all the White paramedics he saw on TV. He hadn't necessarily developed a negative self-image, but he had become aware of White privilege.

Children's race-related questions and observations often go unanswered because the adults in their lives don't know how to respond. Their questions don't go away, but they do gradually learn that race is a taboo topic to discuss. Tatum has endeavored to talk openly with her children about race. When Jonathan asked her why their family was not living in Africa like their ancestors, she explained slavery in a way a four-year-old could understand. She was careful to show that Black people were not merely passive victims of slavery, nor were all White people victimizers. When reading books or watching movies with her children, she pointed out if they were sexist, racist, or otherwise oppressive. Her children learned how to critically examine the media they consume, which better equipped them to resist oppressive messages.

It is also important to surround children with positive images. Tatum made sure that her children had dolls which looked like them and books with Black characters. Historical children's books should not just show White people as the oppressors, but White people who resisted injustice as well. Black communities should show acceptance for Black people of all skin colors. Many grow up in families in which lighter skin colors and straight hair are more desirable—a form of internalized oppression known as colorism. Importantly, children should know that change is possible, and that they too have a voice. A group of second graders in Massachusetts did exactly that when they successfully petitioned their state government to change a sign that was offensive to American Indians.

Chapter 4 Summary: "Identity Development in Adolescence"

Psychologists William and Binta Cross view racial identity as inextricably tied to a person's ethnic and cultural identity as well, known as the racial-ethnic-cultural (REC) identity model. Prior to puberty, a young Black person has not yet undertaken an examination of their REC identity. But as they reach adolescence, their REC group membership becomes increasingly salient to them because "the world begins to reflect their Blackness back to them more clearly" (135). In comparison to their White peers, young Black people are more likely to think of themselves in terms of race because that is how others think of them.

This new awareness of their REC identity tends to be triggered by an event, or a series of smaller events, in which adolescents are forced to acknowledge racism and how it affects them. Tatum gives the example of Malcolm X, who told his junior high school teacher that he wanted to be a lawyer when he grew up. His teacher told him that it wasn't a "realistic goal for a nigger" (139) and to consider carpentry instead. While teachers today are not likely to use the n-word, Black youth continue to receive similar messages. A male Black student recalls a teacher telling him to consider going to community college, despite recommending four-year colleges to the other students in the class. A young Black woman was told by a well-intentioned teacher that she should attend the school dance, because "you people love to dance" (140). Over half of adolescents of color have been targeted by racist attacks online. At racially mixed schools, Black students are far more likely to be placed in less rigorous classes than their White peers even when they achieve similar scores on standardized tests. All of these experiences send a message that the world devalues Blackness.

As Black adolescents become aware of the systematic devaluation and exclusion of Black people, some of them develop an oppositional social identity, which "protects one's identity from the psychological assault of racism and keeps the dominant group at a distance" (143). "Acting White" is viewed negatively, while anything "authentically Black" is valued. At schools where advanced classes are disproportionately White, academic success is often seen as a "White" behavior. Academically successful Black students may be rejected as "not really Black" by their Black peers, while at the same time they struggle to fit in with their White classmates. They may try to become "raceless," in which they de-emphasize their Blackness in order to be accepted. Others adopt an "emissary" identity, in which they see their own successes as successes for all Black people. However, many Black students may feel pressured to always perform well at school due to a condition known as stereotype threat, in which they feel threatened by the thought of inadvertently confirming a negative stereotype, such as the stereotype of Black people being intellectually inferior. This added pressure can end up hindering their academic performance.

So why do the Black kids tend to sit together in the cafeteria? Because their experiences with racism cause them to seek support from people who can understand what they've gone through. While it's important to have a supportive peer group, adults can also play a vital role in supporting Black adolescents. At one middle school in Massachusetts, the school administration set up group meetings for Black students to attend, at which they could talk with teachers about the racial and personal issues that were impeding their academic performance. To lessen the impact of stereotype threat, teachers can communicate to their Black students that they have high expectations for them, and that they also believe that they can meet those expectations. They can promote a view of intelligence as malleable and changeable over time, something that can be improved with effort. Both family members and teachers can actively seek to educate themselves about Black achievements and pass on what they learn to the next generation. Students are less likely to associate academic success with Whiteness if they have Black role models who can help them to "expand their definition of what it means to be Black" (151).

Chapter 5 Summary: "Racial Identity in Adulthood"

When she attended college, Tatum's social circle consisted of fellow Black students. She took classes on African

American history and culture, she stopped straightening her hair, and she sat at the Black table in the dining hall. Many other Black college students go through a similar exploration of their REC identity, during which time they unlearn many of the negative stereotypes they had internalized, while affirming a positive sense of Black identity. At predominantly White universities, Black student unions and cultural centers provide safe spaces where students can feel socially connected and seek support when they are targeted by racism on campus. This period of exploration often involves turning inward—away from dominant group, such that Tatum rarely thought much about White people during her college years—but the individual is often left with a willingness to reach across group boundaries. Identity development involves isolating and exploring a single dimension of who we are, and then reintegrating it into the rest of our identity. This is a process that continues throughout our lives, making us "works in progress for a lifetime" (179).

This process of identity development does not just happen on college campuses. Malcolm X undertook an examination of Black identity while in prison, which included becoming a member of the Nation of Islam (which he later left). The Nation of Islam has offered numerous Black men a positive definition of Blackness, while Black women come together and create positive identities in churches, sororities, and other communities. However, Tatum emphasizes that not all Black adults experience identity development the same way. Some may never actively explore their REC identity. Some may focus more on another dimension of their identity, such as their gender or their religion. Some may adopt a "raceless" persona as they try to conform to White culture. Some may speak openly about racial issues and are race-conscious when raising their children.

Even in corporate cafeterias, Black people can often be seen sitting together, since adults also need to connect with people who share similar experiences. But why do White people ask this question at all? Why do they focus on the group of Black people sitting together? In predominantly White settings, Black people stand out. No one would remark on a group of White people sitting together in the cafeteria, but when Black people do so, White people take notice. They become self-conscious about their race and may worry that they are being excluded, but meanwhile many of them are unaware of how stressful it is to be a member of an underrepresented group. Some companies have made an effort to organize opportunities for marginalized groups—such as people of color, women, people with disabilities, and LGBTQ individuals—to come together and provide each other with some much-needed support.

Part 2 Analysis

As they go through life, the ways in which Black people think of themselves and of White people changes. Children have not yet developed an awareness of their REC identity, but they do begin to internalize White privilege. As they reach puberty, they become increasingly aware that being Black marks them as an "other" in American society. They receive messages which devalue and exclude them. Black adolescents and adults may de-emphasize their Blackness to try to fit in with their White peers, or they may actively disassociate themselves from them. They may simply pay no attention to White people as they undertake an examination of their Black identity, and they may become open to dialogue and friendships across racial boundaries. There is no one way that Black people experience the process of identity development, but race and racism are likely to figure prominently in their lives no matter what.

Throughout these chapters, Tatum highlights the importance of talking about racial issues at all stages of a person's life. Young children begin to have questions about race and differences in physical appearance, and it is important that the adults in their lives answer their questions instead of avoiding them. Black children and adolescents benefit from reading books with characters that look like them, from learning about the many and varied achievements of Black people, and from hearing affirmative messages about their REC group. These positive messages can provide a buffer against the negative messages they will inevitably be exposed to throughout their lives. As they begin to take notice of the racist society they live in, adolescents need to have supportive peers and adults that they can talk to about their experiences. College students and working adults also benefit from having a same-race peer group that in which they can feel safe. Adults who have achieved a positive sense of Black identity are likely to feel a greater sense of inner security than those who seek affirmation from White people.

Tatum also highlights the harm that can come from not having that dialogue or support. If parents and teachers avoid a child's questions about race, then the child will gradually learn to stop asking those questions and will stay confused. Adolescents who are not taught about Black achievements may continue operating with a narrow definition of Blackness, seeing academic success as something for White people. Adults who lack a supportive group of same-race peers may feel alienated and depressed as they have to handle the burden of racism alone. At all stages of life, the answer is not to ignore racial issues.

That doesn't mean that talking about racial issues is easy. How can a parent explain to their 4-year-old why their family is not living in Africa like their ancestors? How can a teacher teach their students about Black history and culture when their own education was limited to learning about Martin Luther King, Jr. and Rosa Parks? While this book does not attempt to provide all the answers, there are some specific examples in these chapters that can provide some guidance for readers. Many parents would be daunted at the prospect of trying to explain slavery to a young child, so Tatum provides an excerpt of how she herself explained it to her son. Teachers who are wondering how they can support Black students may draw inspiration from the example set by the Massachusetts school described in Chapter 4, or from the strategies that Tatum recommends for reducing stereotype threat. Working professionals may consider setting up meetings at their workplace at which employees from underrepresented groups can support each other, as Tatum describes in Chapter 5. There are a number of concrete examples in these pages that readers could potentially apply in their own lives.

Part 3

Part 3: "Understanding Whiteness in a White Context"

Chapter 6 Summary: "The Development of White Identity"

Many White people grow up without thinking or talking much about their own race. As one White author explains, she used to think of people of color as the "real races," while she thought of Whiteness as "plain, normal, the [race] against which all others were measured" (186). This initial stage is known as the contact frame of mind within psychologist Janet Helms' model of White identity development. At this stage, White people are unlikely to have recognized the existence of White privilege or systemic racism, and they often see themselves as free of prejudice. Some may go their entire lives without ever exploring what it means to be White.

The disintegration frame of mind emerges if a White person experiences something that triggers a growing awareness of racism. One White student saw how her Puerto Rican roommate was followed around in stores. For another White woman, watching the video of Philando Castile being killed by a police officer forced her to confront the reality of racism. This new awareness of the pervasiveness of racism tends to lead to uncomfortable feelings of guilt and anger. Their discomfort may cause some people to withdraw—effectively closing their eyes and ears to racism in order to make their discomfort go away—or it could inspire them to take action. They may fervently try to educate their friends and family, only to end up feeling alienated when those around them show little desire to change. To relieve their discomfort, some White people may become angry and blame people of color for the existence of racism, a frame of mind called reintegration. If people of color did something to cause racism, then the White person no longer feels responsible for doing anything about it.

White people may resist being seen as a member of a group, rather than as an individual. The notion that they have systematic advantages due to their race can be difficult to accept when a person believes that they have worked hard to earn things in life, or when they experience a different form of oppression because they are poor, or Jewish, or LGBTQ. As their awareness of systemic racism deepens, they may reach a pseudo-independent mindset— they are committed to unlearning racism, but they don't know what to do about it. They feel guilty about being White and may try to escape their Whiteness by associating with people of color.

The immersion/emersion status is marked by a positive sense of White identity. When a White person redefines Whiteness in a way that "take[s] them beyond the role of victimizer" (201), they can overcome the shame they feel about their race. It is important for them to have antiracist White role models who can serve as a guide—who can show White people that they are not alone, and that they too can make a difference. Tatum provides examples such as Morris Dees, Mab Segrest, and Virginia Foster Durr. There are numerous White individuals who have stood up to racism, yet their stories are rarely taught in school. White people can also join all-White antiracist support groups in which they can make mistakes and work through their feelings of guilt in the company of supportive same-race peers. The final status, autonomy, is achieved when a White person has internalized their redefinition of Whiteness and feels equipped to oppose racism in their daily life.

Chapter 7 Summary: "White Identity, Affirmative Action, and Color-Blind Racial Ideology"

Many White people are resistant to affirmative action programs, believing that they are no longer necessary. They think that people of color no longer face significant barriers, and instead they fear that they themselves are being discriminated against for being White. Statistics show that racial inequality is still very much a problem for people of color, given that there are significant disparities in housing, education, employment, the justice system, healthcare, and other areas. Yet for working-class White Americans in particular, there is the perception that Black people, women, immigrants, and others are "cutting in line" while their own economic situation worsens.

There are a number of misunderstandings about what affirmative action programs are and how they work. They are not quotas, Tatum emphasizes, which in most cases are illegal. Some universities and employers use process-oriented programs, which attempt to make a fair application process. The idea is that if the process is unbiased, then all applicants will be treated fairly. Unfortunately, this often does not work well in practice. Numerous studies have shown that Black and Latinx job applicants receive fewer callbacks from employers than equally qualified White applicants.

Often the problem lies in what psychologists Samuel Gaertner and John Dovidio call "aversive racism." Many White Americans see themselves as racially tolerant and they do not discriminate against anyone in situations where they know what kind of behavior is expected. But in situations that are more ambiguous, their prejudice can emerge. Gaertner and Dovidio showed this in several studies in which they asked White participants to make hiring decisions about Black and White applicants. When one candidate was clearly more qualified, their decisions showed no racial bias. When the choice was less clear, however, they were much more willing to give the benefit of the doubt to White rather than Black candidates. Even though these biases are unconscious and unintentional, the result is nevertheless discriminatory behavior.

A closely related concept is what sociologist Eduardo Bonilla-Silva calls "color-blind racism," in which White people minimize the existence of racial inequality. They may believe that inequalities are due to other factors (such as believing that Black culture is to blame for any hardships that Black people experience), and they tend to be reluctant to talk about race (assuming that if it isn't brought up, then it isn't an issue). Color blindness thus stifles conversations about racial issues and allows the status quo to continue, because "you can't fix what you can't talk about" (228).

Process-oriented affirmative action programs are well intentioned, but they are unlikely to actually give every candidate a fair shot. Goal-oriented programs take a different approach by instead setting diversity goals. Qualified candidates who can help the organization meet those goals are favored in some cases, although White people are still selected sometimes as well. An employer can also establish selection criteria that people of color are more likely to meet, such as experience working in multiracial and multicultural settings. Tatum argues that diversity should be a priority for organizations, not least of all because the organizations themselves benefit from being diverse.

Part 3 Analysis

These two chapters explore some of the mindsets held by White Americans, many of which contribute to the maintenance of racism. They may have difficulty accepting the existence of White privilege because it seems to deny that they worked hard for what they have. Working-class White people in particular may have a hard time seeing how they are privileged because they are at the same time disadvantaged due to their socioeconomic status. They may resent that people of color benefit from affirmative action programs while they themselves struggle financially. Many White Americans would emphatically reject any suggestion that they are prejudiced, yet their prejudices emerge without them being aware that they are discriminating against anyone. Even if a White person recognizes the existence of racial inequality, it doesn't necessarily mean they will become antiracist. Due to the narrative of equal opportunity that they have internalized, they may believe that people of color are at fault for their disadvantages. Many of these mindsets either render systemic racism invisible to White people, or they allow it to be explained away. In either case, the status quo is maintained.

If a White person does challenge the status quo, they will likely find themselves struggling with feelings of guilt and isolation. In Chapter 6, Tatum provides a number of excerpts from narratives written by White people, many of them her own students. These excerpts provide an intimate look into the discomfort they feel with being White, the pain of feeling alienated from their own families, and the empowerment they find when they are able to redefine their Whiteness in a positive way.

While the challenge for Black Americans is to resist the negative messages about their group, the challenge for White Americans is to unlearn racism and resist the social pressure to simply ignore it. Both share a goal in common, however: to develop a positive racial identity. For both Black and White people, having same-race role models can aid them in this endeavor. Having academically successful Black role models can help young Black people expand their definition of Blackness beyond mere stereotypes. White people also benefit from having antiracist White role models who can help them to think of their racial group not just as oppressors, but as people who resist oppression. Black people benefit from having a same-race peer group who they can go to for support, and White people can also benefit from having antiracist White peers who can help them to feel less alone. For both Black and White people, attaining a positive racial identity can make them more effective at cross-racial dialogue. While the challenges they face may be different, there are a number of parallels between Black and White identity development.

Part 4: "Beyond Black and White"

Chapter 8 Summary: "Critical Issues in Latinx, Native, Asian and Pacific Islander, and Middle Eastern / North African Identity Development"

As with Black adolescents, experiences with racism play a fundamental role in the identity development of other adolescents of color. Psychologist Jean Phinney's ethnic identity development model consists of three phrases: unexamined ethnic identity, ethnic identity search, and achieved ethnic identity. As with Black and White people, the identity search is often triggered by an encounter with racism.

Latinxs are now the largest population of color in the United States, but they are an extremely heterogeneous group. About two-thirds are of Mexican ancestry, with the first Mexican Americans becoming a part of US society against their will after the end of the Mexican-American War in 1848. Puerto Ricans were similarly forced to become US citizens following the Spanish-American War in 1898. Cubans, Salvadorans, and people of many other national origins have immigrated to the US throughout the 20th and 21st centuries, driven by economic conditions, political factors, natural disasters, violence, or other reasons. As heterogeneous as they are, Latinxs are to a large extent unified by some shared cultural values, such as familism. In contrast to White Americans, Latinxs tend to be more family oriented and feel a stronger sense of obligation to support their family members. Young Latinxs growing up in US society have to contend with a conflict between their home culture and the dominant culture. They may try to assimilate into the dominant culture, or they may avoid it as much as possible. They may try to bridge the two by being bicultural, but this may also result in not being fully accepted in either one.

Language is also central to many Latinxs' identity, with Spanish being spoken by most (though not all). Some children may feel ashamed that they speak Spanish and so they avoid using it, a result of the negative societal messages which devalue the language. Schools may contribute to this process by treating their native language as a barrier to learning rather than a resource. As they grow older and undertake an examination of their ethnic identity, they may actively reclaim their Spanish. Although the great majority of Latinxs are US citizens or documented immigrants, they can also be affected by the stereotype that they are "illegals." For those who are undocumented, their status can be a source of immense stress and fear. Some parents try to protect their children by not telling them that they are undocumented, which can result in despair and isolation when they eventually learn that they can't apply for college or jobs (the Deferred Action for Childhood Arrivals program, or DACA, has provided a way out of such a situation for many young immigrants since its creation in 2012).

Like Latinxs, Native Americans are a diverse population, consisting of 567 cultural communities. In the centuries following the arrival of Europeans in North America, an estimated 90 percent of Native Americans died from diseases. More were killed in military conflicts and forced relocations. In the 19th and early 20th centuries, American Indian children were taken from their families and put in boarding schools, where they suffered from abuse and forced assimilation. In the 1940s and 1950s, the government relocated many Indians to urban areas, which caused alcoholism, suicide, and homicide rates to skyrocket. In the words of one Native woman, they are "survivors or multigenerational loss" (260). In the present day, American Indians are stereotyped in the media and used as mascots of schools and sports teams. Not only are these portrayals demeaning, but young Native Americans grow up with a very narrow range of images of their own group. In recent decades, some organizations have made an effort to portray a broader range of images and to emphasize that Native people are "not a relic of the past but a growing community with a future" (268).

Asian Americans and Pacific Islander Americans similarly consist of people who come from a multitude of different backgrounds, but their group identity has been made possible because the dominant culture treats them as the same, and they therefore have similar experiences with racism. Chinese immigrants have resided in the US since the 19th century and were frequently targets of bigotry and violence. Japanese immigrants similarly have a long history in the US and were targeted by anti-Japanese sentiment in the wake of Pearl Harbor in 1941, resulting in many being incarcerated in internment camps. The 1965 Immigration Act abolished racial quotas and paved the way for increased levels of immigration, including people from China, Korea, the Philippines, India, and other countries. After the end of the Vietnam War in 1975, a number of refugees from Southeast Asia also made their way to the US. Others became a part of US society by colonization rather than migration, particularly Native Hawaiian and Pacific Islanders.

Asian Americans are frequently stereotyped as the "model minority" who are academically and economically successful. Some groups who immigrate from Asia to the US disproportionately consist of people who are highly educated, which has created the perception that Asian

Americans in general are highly educated as well. For Asian American students, this can sometimes become a "self-fulfilling prophecy" (280) in that they do well at school because everyone expects it of them. For other students, it can mean feeling like a failure and becoming distanced from their ethnic community—feeling like they aren't "Vietnamese enough" or not "authentically Korean" (281)—because they haven't achieved the high standards set for them. The model minority stereotype is also harmful in that it obscures the reality that Asian Americans are also targets of racism.

Americans have the tendency to categorize people from the Middle East and North Africa (MENA) as Arab or Muslim, but the reality is that they are an ethnically and religiously heterogeneous group. Regardless of whether they are actually Arab or Muslim, the MENA population has been stereotyped as "terrorists" in the years since 9/11 attacks. The hostility toward Islam has had a profound effect on young Muslims, with one student saying it was exhausting to "constantly feel that you have to be on the defensive and justify who you are" (290). Author Amani al-Khatahtbeh described the shame she felt when she denied being Muslim as a child, and the empowerment she found when she finally decided to reclaim her identity. Feelings of isolation can be reduced by having Muslim friends to connect with, and non-Muslims can also make a difference by helping them feel like they belong. Tatum suggests that educators can support their MENA and Muslim students by educating themselves, by vocally opposing Islamophobia, and by making sure they feel included in the school community.

Chapter 9 Summary: "Identity Development in Multiracial Families"

The identity development of multiracial children depends on a wide array of factors, including (but not limited to) which races are involved, the physical appearance of the child, the family situation, and the environment they live in. While there are of course many racial combinations, Tatum mainly focuses in this chapter on children of one Black parent and one White parent. Historically, the "one-drop rule" meant that anyone with any Black ancestry was classified as Black, even if their appearance was wholly that of a White person. It was a practice that "solidified the boundary between Black and White" (301). Today, racially ambiguous people may frequently hear the question, "What are you?" People seek to racially classify them as their existence challenges those racial boundaries.

Sociologists Kerry Ann Rockquemore and David Brunsma conducted a large-scale study of how Black-White biracial people understand who they are. Some develop a singular identity, either identifying exclusively as Black or exclusively as White. Those with a Black identity are often assumed to be Black based on their appearance, and so they identify as Black because it is how society treats them. Michelle, on the other hand, is one of the 3 percent of participants who identify as exclusively White. She is perceived by society as White and she lives in an almost entirely White community. She is open about the fact that her father is Black, but Blackness is not a part of her own identity.

The majority of participants have a border identity, in which they don't think of themselves as Black or White, but as a separate category which incorporates both. Sometimes this identity is validated by others, as is the case for Anthony, who is racially ambiguous and attends a school with many other biracial students. Other times their identity is not validated, as is the case for Chris. Although she identifies as biracial, others assume she is Black based on her appearance. A small number of participants have a protean identity, who are "multicultural 'border-crossers,' shifting from one identity to another with relative ease" (312). The remainder have a transcendent identity in which they simply do not see themselves in terms of race and refuse to assign themselves to a racial category.

While physical appearance plays a role in the identity development process, the parents also play a highly significant role. They make decisions on where their child lives and attends school, which in turn affect whether the children have access to racially mixed social networks. Some parents may provide their child with positive messages about their Black heritage, while others may devalue it. Some may encourage a biracial identity by providing their child with positive exposure to both Black and White social groups, while others with a color-blind ideology may not want to talk about racial issues at all. The lack of dialogue on race and racism can particularly impact children of color who are adopted by White parents, since they lack an adult of color in their family. They may end up feeling alienated from White people because their physical appearance sets them apart, yet not accepted within their racial or ethnic group because of their lack of cultural knowledge. Tatum emphasizes that before adopting a child of color, White parents should be prepared to talk about racial issues and to accompany their child as they navigate their encounters with racism.

Part 4 Analysis

Throughout these two chapters, Tatum repeatedly emphasizes the heterogeneity of the groups that she discusses. There is no single way that multiracial people experience being multiracial, and there is a great amount of diversity among Latinxs, Native Americans, Asian Americans, Pacific Islander Americans, Muslims, and people of MENA heritage. They have different national origins, they come from different socioeconomic and ethnic backgrounds, they have different religions, they have different cultures, they speak different languages, and they migrate for different reasons (or in some cases, they became a part of US society through colonization). Even those who come from the same country can have very different experiences, such as the light-skinned upper-class Cuban immigrants who came to the US shortly after the Cuban Revolution, versus the dark-skinned impoverished Cuban immigrants who came later. When people are grouped under a single label—whether it's "Latinx," "Cuban," or any other label—it can have homogenizing consequences. It can oversimplify people who identify with the group and erase their internal differences. In an attempt to counteract such assumptions, Tatum is careful to note that each of these groups is far more diverse than can possibly be captured in the space of a few chapters.

Although some of these groups do have other characteristics in common, such as certain cultural values, the main thing that unites them is racism. If Asian Americans are perceived as the same by the dominant culture, then they will have similar experiences with racism, and the same goes for other groups. As Tatum discussed in Chapter 1, the dominant group is often ignorant about the subordinate groups. In this ignorance, harmful stereotypes are allowed to flourish: Latinxs are seen as "illegal" immigrants, Native Americans are seen as a "relic of the past" (268), Asian Pacific Americans are seen as quiet and content with the status quo, and Arabs and Muslims (who are believed to be one and the same) are seen as "terrorists".

There are many parts in these chapters that provide a look into the history of racism in the US. Chinese immigrants in the 19th century were reviled for supposedly ruining the economy, not unlike how immigrants today (and particularly Latinx immigrants) are accused of stealing jobs. Japanese Americans were labeled the enemy after the bombing of Pearl Harbor, which bears a resemblance to the heightened bigotry aimed at Muslims, Arabs, and people of MENA ancestry in the years since 9/11. The one-drop rule meant that people were considered Black if they had any Black ancestry, and today Black-White biracial people are still likely to be treated by society as simply Black. These parallels between history and the modern day are a reminder that although many things have changed, not everything has changed. Racism continues to have a pervasive presence.

When it comes to the identity development of the groups discussed in these chapters, many of the key takeaways are the same as in previous sections. An exploration of one's racial or ethnic identity often begins by having an encounter with racism. The challenge is then to overcome the negative societal messages about one's own group and to find a positive sense of group identity. The pain of feeling isolated and marginalized can be reduced by having same-group peers to rely on for support and by having allies who publicly voice their support as well.

Part 5: "Breaking the Silence"

Chapter 10 Summary: "Embracing a Cross-Racial Dialogue"

Some Americans feel there is already too much talk about racial issues, but Tatum argues that we need much more. Many White people avoid talking about racism out of fear of becoming isolated from friends and family, fear of being rejected by others who don't like what they say, or fear of exposing their own ignorance by saying the wrong thing. People of color can also be afraid to talk about racism. It can be terrifying to broach the subject without knowing how others will respond. Sometimes there is the fear that speaking up will accomplish nothing, leaving them angry and frustrated once again. Both White people and people of color need to overcome their fears and take the risk of speaking up.

For a person of color, staying silent can mean internalizing one's own oppression. They may deny their experiences with racism and place the blame on themselves. For a White person, the pressure to not notice racism means that their own racial identity and privilege are left unexamined. Breaking the silence can be empowering, but it also takes courage to push past the fear. Tatum recommends for each person to focus on their own sphere of influence. Parents and teachers can think of the conversations they have with their children or students. Anyone can reach out to newspapers or broadcasters to contribute their opinions. Employers can think about who is underrepresented in their workforce. Athletes can think about how they talk and behave around their teammates. None of us are perfect and we will all inevitably make mistakes—Tatum herself acknowledges that she has made many mistakes throughout her life—but we all must begin to speak. Even though words are not enough, they are a necessary first step to producing change.

Epilogue Summary: "Signs of Hope, Sites of Progress"

While the Prologue discussed how little progress has been made in the past 20 years, that doesn't mean that there is no good news at all. Some people do speak up about racism within their sphere of influence. Tatum highlights one instance in which a university class president, a White man, publicly challenged those who stayed silent following a racist incident on campus. Throughout the Epilogue, Tatum highlights a number of initiatives that have been effective at producing meaningful change. Many of them are small in scale but have shown promising results that could be applied elsewhere.

One such program is the Atlanta Friendship Initiative, which creates friendship pairs between two people of different races or ethnicities. Participants have said that the conversations they have had with their partner have taught them a great deal. Another is The Welcome Table, a program at the William Winter Institute which facilitates trust building and storytelling activities among people of different racial backgrounds. Educational institutions can also play a vital role by helping students develop the capacity to listen to one another. At the University of Michigan, students have the option of taking intergroup dialogue courses, which foster meaningful encounters between people of different backgrounds. Dialogue programs have begun to spread to other institutions as well. While things may not be better now than they were 20 years ago, Tatum is hopeful that we can make the future better.

Part 5 Analysis

In comparison to much of the rest of the book, and the Prologue in particular, Tatum ends the book on a much more hopeful note. Reading about the pervasiveness of racism in American society is likely to make many readers feel hopeless, but Tatum's goal is to inspire them to take action and produce change, and for that it is necessary to have hope for the future. She acknowledges that many readers are likely afraid, but she encourages them to push past their fears, as many other activists have done throughout history.

Even if they find the courage to speak up, many readers may feel that they are not powerful enough to make a difference. Tatum emphasizes that small changes are significant. We each have our own sphere of influence at home, at school, at work, or elsewhere. We may not individually be able to change institutional policies and practices, but the small changes that we make within our own social circles can lead to bigger societal changes.

Beverly Daniel Tatum

Beverly Daniel Tatum is a clinical psychologist specializing in racial identity development who has also held leadership positions in higher education, including serving as the president of Spelman College for 13 years. In her career as an educator, she found a sense of purpose in teaching her students about the significance of racial identity, how racism operates in society, and what can be done about racism. Believing that others could benefit from this knowledge as well, Tatum has given numerous talks and written several books which contribute a psychological perspective to the public discourse on racial issues.

In addition to her expertise in racial identity development, Tatum also draws heavily on her own life experiences throughout this book. She includes stories about growing up as a young Black woman in a predominantly White community as well as stories about raising two Black sons. She also discusses the things she has learned from working with her racially and ethnically diverse students over the years. Many of her students' narratives about their own experiences are featured in this book.

White as "Normal," Color as "Other"

People of color receive messages throughout their lives that they are different, that they are worth less, that they are abnormal, that they don't belong. Asian Pacific Americans are assumed to be foreign, even when they were born in the US. Black Americans receive messages at school that they are less intelligent and capable of achieving less. Latinxs are treated as outsiders for speaking Spanish, Muslims are rejected for believing in a "violent" and "hateful" religion, and Native people are reduced to caricatures in the media. Parents of White children can easily find countless children's books with White characters, while Tatum had to actively search for books and toys that reflected her sons' appearances. In recent years, Trump's polarizing discourse has only served to further emphasize that people of color are "them" and not "us." As a result of all these messages, young people of color become increasingly aware as they grow up that their race or ethnicity marks them as an "other."

One result of otherness is increased visibility. As they go about their lives, people of color are continuously seen as members of their group, whereas White people are accustomed to being seen simply as individuals. White people therefore take notice if a group of Black people are sitting together in the cafeteria, but not if a group of White people are sitting together. This constant feeling of otherness can be immensely stressful but having a group of peers from the same racial or ethnic group can help a person to feel less isolated.

Sometimes, however, people of color feel like outsiders both among White people *and* among people from the same racial or ethnic group. Latinxs who aren't proficient in Spanish may find themselves rejected by other White people for being Latinx, but also rejected by other Spanish-speaking Latinxs. Asian Pacific Americans who don't meet high standards of academic achievement may feel like they don't belong among their group because they feel like "failures." Children of color who are adopted into White families may be treated as an "other" by their White peers, but may grow up to feel like they don't belong among their racial or ethnic group either because of their lack of linguistic or cultural knowledge.

White people, on the other hand, often just think of themselves as "normal"—a problematic belief, since it implies that anyone who isn't White is "abnormal." They may believe that they treat all people equally without regard for their race, but nevertheless send othering messages without realizing it. People of color may try to fit in with White people by trying to become "raceless"—by de-emphasizing their Blackness, by abandoning their Spanish, by denying their religion—but this often leaves a person uncomfortable because they are denying a part of who they are. Ultimately, being treated as others is what causes people of color to develop their group identity. Although the dominant culture devalues them, people of color can reject the negative messages and embrace a positive redefinition of who they are.

White Ignorance

Many White Americans are ignorant about a lot of things when it comes to race and racism. The majority of White people have entirely White social circles, so they are ignorant about what it is like to be a person of color. The media portrays people of color as one-dimensional stereotypes and they probably didn't learn much about people of color at school either, so they are ignorant about their histories, cultures, and diversity. They were raised to be "color-blind," to believe that talking about race or racism is impolite—or even racist—and so they stay silent about it. In this silence, they believe that racism is a problem of the past and not of the present.

White ignorance is harmful for people of color. Because White people remain ignorant of institutional and cultural racism, they maintain these discriminatory systems. They may perpetuate painful stereotypes and misinformation in their daily conversations, and their implicit biases may reveal themselves in their actions even while they believe they are completely without prejudice. The problem is not that there is a lack of evidence available about racism, but that their mindset encourages them to ignore it or explain it away—and this can include failing to listen when a person of color speaks up about racism. Staying ignorant is a way to maintain their psychological comfort.

While the harm is greater for people of color, White people themselves are also harmed by their own ignorance. They are likely to feel uncomfortable in their interactions with people of color. They may feel hurt that they are not able to connect or form friendships with them, and they may not even understand why, since they are ignorant of their own ignorance as well. When racism is so pervasive in American society, it takes an active effort to not notice it, and Tatum claims this continuous effort to avoid acknowledging racism can leave White people ignorant about themselves:

> But in not noticing, one loses opportunities for greater insight into oneself and one's experience. A significant dimension of who one is in the world, one's Whiteness, remains uninvestigated and

perceptions of daily experience are routinely distorted. Privilege goes unnoticed, and all but the most blatant acts of racial bigotry are ignored. Not noticing requires energy. (338)

White identity development involves overcoming this ignorance. They begin to recognize the presence of racism, they reeducate themselves about the stereotypes they internalized and the things they never learned, and they learn how to listen. Part of this process involves overcoming their fear of speaking up, since they are often afraid of revealing their own ignorance. Confronting one's own ignorance can be frightening, but it can make them effective allies who can engage in cross-racial dialogues with mutual respect.

The Necessity of Dialogue and the Cost of Silence

We are a "color-silent" society, according to Tatum. We see race and it affects our daily lives, but many Americans avoid talking about it or thinking about it. Many are silent about racism because they believe it is only a problem when it is talked about out loud. Fear is also a silencing force, with many White people staying silent because they're afraid of saying the wrong thing, while people of color may stay silent because they're afraid their words will be ignored. Parents may silence their children when they ask questions about race, or avoid talking to them about racism out of fear that they will introduce problems where there were none before. Children may grow up learning to stay silent about racism themselves, and thus the silence is passed down from one generation to the next.

Silence comes with some heavy costs. Children of color may be unprepared to handle their encounters with racism, and they may internalize the negative messages about their own group if no one provides them with positive messages. White people's silence allows for them to continue to not notice institutional and cultural racism, even while Black people are dying at the hands of police officers before their eyes. Staying passively silent means that the actively hateful are permitted to voice their hate, as was described in the words of one White university student following a racist incident on his campus:

> I feel that silence in response to these comments camouflages the genuinely hateful and empowers them in the development of their beliefs. [...] Our silence fosters hate. Our silence enables the hateful to feel comfortable and welcome. (344)

As difficult and frightening as it may be to talk about racism, it is imperative that we do so. We each have a sphere of influence in which we can break the silence. Parents need to answer their children's questions, teach them about oppression and how to resist it, and provide them with affirmative messages about their own group. We need dialogues within our own racial or ethnic groups to emotionally support each other and help each other to find a positive identity. We need dialogues across our different groups to foster empathy and mutual respect. We need to speak out against racism publicly and frequently. Words alone may not be enough, but they can achieve a lot.

Active and Passive Racism

In Chapter 1, Tatum draws a distinction between active and passive racism. While the former consists of "blatant, intentional acts of racial bigotry and discrimination" (91), the latter consists of more subtle acts, such as laughing at a racist joke or staying silent about exclusionary policies or practices. Although one is more obvious than the other, they both support the maintenance of racism.

Affirmative Action

Affirmative action programs are one of the main focuses of Chapter 7. Public universities and employers with federal contracts are required to "develop procedures that [...] result in equal employment opportunity for historically disadvantaged groups" (215), including people of color, women, people with disabilities, and veterans. Some institutions develop process-oriented affirmative action programs, which attempt to create an unbiased application process. Tatum argues that these are often not effective because people make biased decisions even when they don't intend to. Goal-oriented programs, on the other hand, set diversity goals and continually evaluate whether they are making progress toward those goals.

Aversive Racism

Psychologists Samuel Gaertner and John Dovidio claim that many White Americans are "aversive racists", which is a result of them "internaliz[ing] the espoused cultural values of fairness and justice for all *at the same time* that they have been breathing the smog of racial biases and stereotypes pervading popular culture" (220). Aversive racists see themselves as racially tolerant, but they are often uncomfortable interacting with people of color. They are resistant to the idea that they might be prejudiced, but their racial prejudices often emerge in ambiguous situations. Tatum discusses aversive racism in Chapter 7 as a reason why so many White people are opposed to affirmative action.

Color-Blind Racial Ideology

As discussed in Chapter 7, there is a pervasive ideology in the US that sociologist Eduardo Bonilla-Silva refers to as "color-blind racism", in which "White people deny or minimize the degree of racial inequality or explain contemporary racial inequality as the result of factors unrelated to racial dynamics" (226). They often believe that everyone has equal opportunities in life, and so people of color are to blame for any adversities they experience. White people are often reluctant to talk about racial issues, since it is believed that bringing up race is racist in and of itself. This ideology thus stifles dialogue and encourages the maintenance of the status quo.

Colorism

In Black communities, there is sometimes a preference for lighter skin colors over darker skin colors, a form of oppression known as colorism. In Chapter 3, Tatum discusses how colorism within Black families can send negative messages to children.

Internalized Oppression

When surrounded by so many negative messages, some people of color may end up "believing the distorted messages about one's own group" (86). They may deny their experiences with racism, believing that they themselves are to blame. One manifestation of internalized oppression is colorism, which is discussed in Chapter 3.

Microaggressions

Microaggressions are the "daily slights and insults" (51) experienced by people of color as well as other marginalized groups. In the Prologue, Tatum gives some examples of the microaggressions that many Asian Americans experience, such as being told to "go back home." These microaggressions can trigger a growing awareness of racism in adolescents of color.

Oppositional Social Identity

In Chapter 4, Tatum describes how a growing awareness of racism can lead to the development of an oppositional social identity for some Black adolescents. They distance themselves from anything perceived to be "White," while any behaviors that are "authentically Black" are valued. Oftentimes, however, their notions of what is "Black" and what is not are heavily influenced by stereotypes.

Prejudice

Tatum defines prejudice as "a preconceived judgment or opinion, usually based on limited information" (85). While some people are more overtly prejudiced than others, we all inevitably acquire prejudices because of the racist societal messages that surround us, which Tatum compares to a "smog" that we all breathe in. Many Americans view racism and prejudice as the same thing, but Tatum emphasizes that the two are distinct.

Racial and Ethnic Identity Development

Tatum defines racial identity development as "the process of defining for oneself the personal significance and social meaning of belonging to a particular racial group" (96). While a distinction can be drawn between racial identity and ethnic identity (the former based on physical criteria and the latter on cultural criteria), the two frequently intersect. When discussing the racial identity development of Black adolescents in Chapter 4, Tatum uses William and Binta Cross' racial-ethnic-cultural (REC) identity model, which is based on the view that "'racial, ethnic, and cultural identity overlap at the level of lived experience' to the point that there is little reason to discuss them separately" (134).

For White identity development in Chapter 6, Tatum uses Janet Helms' model, which focuses on the "abandonment of individual racism" and subsequently the "recognition of and opposition to institutional and cultural racism" (187). When discussing the identity development of other groups of color in Chapter 8, Tatum uses Jean Phinney's ethnic identity development model, which involves three phases: unexamined identity, identity search, and achieved ethnic identity. All of these models are similar in that an exploration of one's own identity is often precipitated by an encounter with racism, and that a positive self-definition develops over time.

Racism

While many Americans conceive of racism as simply overt expressions of bigotry, this is a limited understanding which excludes cultural and institutional racism. Using sociologist David Wellman's definition, Tatum sees racism as a "system of advantage based on race," which involves "cultural messages and institutional policies and practices as well as the beliefs and actions of individuals" (87). This broader definition emphasizes that White people systematically benefit from racism while people of color are systematically disadvantaged by it.

Stereotype Threat

Tatum discusses stereotype threat in Chapter 4 in relation to the added pressure that Black students may feel to perform well at school. Social psychologist Claude Steele defines it as "the threat of being viewed through the lens of a negative stereotype, or the fear of doing something that would inadvertently confirm that stereotype" (159). Due to the stereotype that Black people are intellectually inferior, Black students may feel pressured to always do well at school in order to disprove the stereotype, but this pressure can end up inhibiting their academic performance.

White Privilege

White privilege refers to the "systematic advantages of being White" (88). The term was popularized by an article written by feminist and antiracist activist Peggy McIntosh in 1989. In her article, McIntosh covers a long list of benefits that White people experience but are largely unaware of as they go about their daily lives.

IMPORTANT QUOTES

1. "It is not just the reality that a Black man could be the president of the United States that has threatened the status quo. It is also the collapse of the American economy in September 2008 and the financial threat that many felt in the waning months of George W. Bush's presidency; it is the ruptured sense of security brought on by the 9/11 terrorist attacks in 2001 and other, more recent attacks on American soil; it is the slow recognition that the United States might not always hold its position of prominence in the world; and perhaps especially it is the fact that White people will soon be the numerical minority in the US. Each of these societal changes represents a challenge to a set of assumptions, deeply held, by many in our nation, and anxiety—even fear—is the result." (Prologue, Pages 21-22)

   Obama's election was widely seen as a sign of social progress, but it was also a change that contributed to the anxiety felt by many White Americans. The fear that society was changing in unpredictable ways can lead to "us versus them" behavior because they feel a loss of control over the direction that society is headed in. These White people lash out at those who they perceive to be "against" them, leading to a rise in hate crimes following the 2008 election. While Obama's presidency did indeed represent progress, that progress does not come easily or without costs.

2. "Yes, we have an innate tendency to think in 'us' and 'them' categories, but we look to the leader to help us know who the 'us' is and who the 'them' is. The leader can define who is in and who is out." (Prologue, Page 70)

Leaders have considerable power over people's
attitudes and beliefs. They have greater access to forms
of public discourse (anything they say is likely to be
widely reported in the media, for example) and their
social position means that people are more likely to
listen to what they have to say. Trump's exclusionary
rhetoric has heightened the fears of many White people
and has led to increased hostility toward people of
color and other marginalized groups.

3. "If you were born in 1997, you were eleven when the
economy collapsed, perhaps bringing new economic
anxiety into your family life. You were still eleven
when Barack Obama was elected. You heard that we
were now in a postracial society and President Obama's
election was the proof. Yet your neighborhoods and
schools were likely still quite segregated. And in 2012,
when you were fifteen, a young Black teenager named
Trayvon Martin, walking home in his father's mostly
White neighborhood with his bag of iced tea and
Skittles, was murdered and his killer went free. When
you were seventeen, Michael Brown was shot in
Ferguson, Missouri, and his body was left uncovered in
the streets for hours, like a piece of roadkill, and in the
same year, unarmed Eric Garner was strangled to death
by police, repeatedly gasping 'I can't breathe' on a viral
cell phone video, to name just two examples of why it
seemed Black lives did not matter, even in the age of
Obama. When you were nineteen, Donald J. Trump was
elected president and White supremacists were
celebrating in the streets. How would a twenty-year-old
answer the question posed to me, 'Is it better?'"
(Prologue, Pages 71-72)

Just because we are moving forward in time does not
mean we are making social progress. This quote, which

comes at the end of the Prologue, reiterates just how
many injustices we have witnessed in first few decades
of the 21st century. These events have shaped young
people, and so it is little wonder that the Black Lives
Matter movement has grown out of their anger. Tatum
highlights all of these setbacks not to overwhelm or
depress readers, but to show them that there is still a lot
of work we need to do as a society.

4. "There is always someone who hasn't noticed the
   stereotypical images of people of color in the media,
   who hasn't observed the housing discrimination in their
   community, who hasn't read the newspaper articles
   about documented racial bias in lending practices
   among well-known banks, who isn't aware of the racial
   tracking pattern at the local school, who hasn't seen the
   reports of rising incidents of racially motivated hate
   crimes in America—in short, someone who hasn't been
   paying attention to issues of race." (Chapter 1, Page 83)

   Tatum provides a long list of the ways that racism exists
   in American society to show that it is not only present,
   it is pervasive. She emphasizes that there is hard
   evidence that cultural and institutional racism exists by
   pointing out that it has been documented in published
   research and official reports. Many White people do
   not fail to see racism because there is a lack of
   evidence, but because they have been raised to not
   notice it. And if they do notice it, as Tatum elaborates
   on later in Chapter 6, there are internal and societal
   pressures to close one's eyes again.

5. "Cultural racism—the cultural images and messages
   that affirm the assumed superiority of Whites and the
   assumed inferiority of people of color—is like smog in
   the air. Sometimes it is so thick it is visible, other times

it is less apparent, but always, day in and day out, we are breathing it in. None of us would introduce ourselves as 'smog breathers' (and most of us don't want to be described as prejudiced), but if we live in a smoggy place, how can we avoid breathing the air?" (Chapter 1, Page 86)

By comparing cultural racism to a "smog," Tatum emphasizes not only the inevitability of acquiring prejudices, but that we aren't personally responsible for becoming prejudiced. Some readers are likely to be resistant to the suggestion that they are prejudiced because it implies that they are at fault, but Tatum shows here that it is simply an unfortunate consequence of being surrounded by such messages. Just as smog is bad for our health, living in a racist society is harmful to us as well.

6. "Unless we engage in these and other conscious acts of reflection and reeducation, we easily repeat the process with our children. The unexamined prejudices of the parents are passed on to the children. It is not our fault, but it is our responsibility to interrupt this cycle." (Chapter 1, Page 87)

In this quote, Tatum emphasizes the cyclical nature of racism—it continues to reproduce itself from one generation to the next unless people make an active effort to stop it. Although it is not our fault that we acquired prejudices, we are at fault if we do nothing about it. To counteract our prejudices, we need to engage in self-introspection and educate ourselves beyond the stereotypes we have learned from the media and the limited information we learned at school.

7. "To the extent that one can draw on one's own experience of subordination—as a young person, as a person with a disability, as someone who grew up poor, as a woman—it may be easier to make meaning of another targeted group's experience. For those readers who are targeted by racism and are angered by the obliviousness of Whites sometimes described in these pages, it may be useful to attend to your experience of dominance where you may find it—as a heterosexual, as an able-bodied person, as a Christian, as a man—and consider what systems of privilege you may be overlooking. The task of resisting our own oppression does not relieve us of the responsibility of acknowledging our complicity in the oppression of others." (Chapter 2, Page 108)

Although this book focuses on racism, it is no more or less significant than the many other forms of oppression that take place as well. Since many people are simultaneously members of dominant as well as subordinate groups, Tatum asks readers to reflect on their own experiences with being both advantaged and disadvantaged. This introspection can aid readers in understanding better what it is like to be White or a person of color, which can help them to have more empathy and patience in their cross-racial dialogues.

8. "Learning to spot 'that stuff'—whether it is racist, or sexist, or classist—is an important skill for children to develop. It is as important for my Black male children to recognize sexism and other forms of oppression as it is for them to spot racism. We are better able to resist the negative impact of oppressive messages when we see them coming than when they are invisible to us." (Chapter 3, Page 126)

Tatum reiterates the importance of recognizing and speaking out against all forms of oppression, not just racism. She also emphasizes the importance of teaching children how to resist oppressive messages. Many parents would shy away from talking about such topics with their children, possibly fearing that they would be needlessly exposing their child to something painful and unpleasant, but children will inevitably be exposed to such messages throughout their lives no matter what. Tatum uses her own family as an example to show that children are capable of developing a critical consciousness and that it can aid them in life, not hinder them.

9. "Why do Black youths, in particular, think about themselves in terms of race? Because that is how the rest of the world thinks of them. Our self-perceptions are shaped by the messages that we receive from those around us, and when young Black men and women enter adolescence, the racial content of those messages intensifies." (Chapter 4, Page 133)

As Tatum also discussed in Chapter 2, the most salient dimensions of our identity are those that the rest of society treats as abnormal. For a young Black person, reaching adolescence is often accompanied by a growing realization that the dominant culture has marked them as an "other." They may be looked down upon or pushed to the margins of society.

10. "Whether it is the experience of being followed in stores because they are suspected of shoplifting, seeing people respond to them with fear on the street, or feeling overlooked in school, Black youth can benefit from seeking support from those who have had similar experiences." (Chapter 4, Page 155)

Young Black people routinely have encounters with racism, but it very often does not take the form of overt bigotry. Here, Tatum gives a few examples of some of the messages that Black adolescents may receive that Blackness is devalued. The question, "Why are all the Black people sitting together in the cafeteria?" is often asked by White people—possibly oblivious to the fact that they themselves may also be contributing to the marginalization that causes Black adolescents to seek support from each other. It is important for Black adolescents to have peers who understand their experiences with racism, and a same-race peer group can provide that emotional support.

11. "She highlights what happens to the O, the token, in a world of Xs. In corporate America, Black people are still in the O position. One consequence of being an O, Kanter points out, is heightened visibility. When an O walks into the room, the Xs notice. Whatever the O does, positive or negative, stands out because of this increased visibility. It is hard for an O to blend in. When several Os are together, the attention of the Xs is really captured. Without the tokens present in the room, the Xs go about their business, perhaps not even noticing that they are all Xs." (Chapter 5, Pages 179-180)

Tatum addresses why the question in the title of this book is even asked in the first place. After all, White people don't notice anything strange if a group of White people are sitting together in a cafeteria. Tatum cites a book by psychologist Rosabeth Moss Kanter which illustrates what it is like to be a "token." Whiteness is taken for granted as "normal" and does not capture the attention of White people, while Blackness is treated as "otherness" and does. Black

*people trying to live, study, or work in predominantly
White settings have to do so while constantly being seen
as Black. Part of White privilege is that people pay no
attention to their race much of the time.*

12. "There is a lot of silence about race in White
communities, and as a consequence Whites tend to
think of racial identity as something that other people
have, not something that is salient for them." (Chapter
6, Page 186)

*This culture of silence among White people means that
they tend to grow up not thinking of themselves as
White, but just as what's "normal". They don't explore
the existence of racism or the privileges they receive for
being White. They learn to not talk about race or
racism from a young age, and by not talking about or
thinking about it, the status quo is maintained.*

13. "We all must be able to embrace who we are in terms of
our racial and cultural heritage, not in terms of assumed
superiority or inferiority but as an integral part of our
daily experience in which we can take pride. But, as we
see in these examples for many White people who have
come to understand the everyday reality of racism,
Whiteness is still experienced as a source of shame
rather than as a source of pride." (Chapter 6, Page 200)

*If a White person overcomes the social pressure to not
notice racism, they often struggle with feelings of guilt
about being White. They see their own group as
oppressors and feel ashamed to belong to such a group.
According to Tatum, one of the challenges for White
people is finding a positive redefinition of what it
means to be White—in other words, seeing their own
group not just as oppressors, but as people who oppose*

oppression.

14. "Another feature of color-blind racial ideology is the belief that talking about race makes things worse—that it promotes racism and/or is racist in and of itself. Those who bring up race are 'playing the race card' and creating problems where otherwise there would be none, or so the logic goes." (Chapter 7, Page 227)

    The pervasive color-blind ideology allows for White people to perceive themselves as non-racist while staying oblivious to the reality of racism. This facet of the ideology, which pressures people to stay silent about race, allows the cycle of racism to continue unimpeded. By not seeing racism and not talking about racism, a White person is able to persist in the belief that the status quo is perfectly fine.

15. "The linguistic, religious, and other cultural diversity of these disparate groups [...] gives validity to the question posed by Valerie Lee, director of the 1992 Asian American Renaissance Conference: 'What do we have in common except for racism and rice?' Social scientists Kenyon Chan and Shirley Hune argue that racism is quite enough. Because the treatment of early Asian immigrant communities was so similar and distinctions between them ignored by the dominant culture, the foundation of a group identity was laid." (Chapter 8, Page 275)

    When discussing each racial and ethnic group throughout Chapter 8, Tatum repeatedly emphasizes the diversity that each group contains. This raises the question of what members of these groups have in common in the first place if they are so diverse—and the answer is, in large part, racism. Asian Americans may have drastically different heritages, but since these differences are disregarded by the dominant culture, they have similar experiences with racism.

16. "Amani's assertion of her identity through the claiming of her head scarf, despite her earlier rejection of it, is reminiscent of the example of the Latina who reclaimed her Spanish and its importance to her identity in college after her childhood rejection of the language that had set her apart from the mainstream, again illustrating the similarity of the process of identity exploration among marginalized groups in the face of that marginalization." (Chapter 8, Page 293)

    Even amongst the diversity of racial and ethnic identities, people of color are affected by racism in remarkably similar ways. Children often try to fit in with their White peers by abandoning anything that symbolically marks them as an "other," such as speaking Spanish or wearing a hijab. As they grow older and reclaim their identity, they may search for visible and symbolic ways to assert it as well. In Amani's case, wearing her hijab was a way to show that she was proud to be Muslim despite being harassed for it as a child.

17. "Anyone can interrupt an offensive joke, challenge stereotypes, or offer assistance to someone who is being harassed or is fearful that they might be. If you don't know how best to be helpful, ask and then *listen*. Use your own privilege to question policies that are discriminatory. Be public in your support for those who are targeted, so they will know where to find help when it is needed. In a time of darkness, we all have to generate more light." (Chapter 8, Page 297)

Tatum encourages readers to publicly support Muslims and people of MENA heritage and offers specific examples of what a person can do in their daily lives to oppose Islamophobia. People who are targeted may often feel marginalized from mainstream society, so vocal and visible support can help to remedy those feelings of isolation. While Tatum is referring to speaking up against Islamophobia in this quote, her words could arguably be applied more broadly to speaking up against any form of oppression.

18. "One such challenge is embodied in the frequently asked question, 'What are you?' While the question may be prompted by the individual's sometimes racially ambiguous appearance, the insistence with which the question is often asked represents society's need to classify its members racially. The existence of the biracial person challenges the rigid boundaries between Black and White, and the questioner may really be asking, 'Which side are you on? Where do you stand?'" (Chapter 9, Page 306)

This quote appears after Tatum's discussion of the "one-drop rule," which was a practice intended to maintain a firm division between Black and White people. While the one-drop rule is no longer used today, the boundary remains, and people may be uncomfortable when someone seems to defy that racial boundary. They may insist on placing a person firmly in one racial category or another.

19. "Parents who have a 'color-blind' ideology may be reluctant to talk to their children about potential encounters with racism, hoping perhaps that if they don't mention it, it won't be a problem. Talking about the possibility of such interactions and providing

children with appropriate responses they might use in such situations is one way to inoculate children against the stress of this kind of racism." (Chapter 9, Page 321)

Tatum emphasizes that it is parents' responsibility to talk with their children about racism. Staying silent does not mean it will go away, it will only mean that children will be unprepared and confused when they encounter it. If parents are too uncomfortable to talk about it, then they are leaving their child to experience the burden of racism alone. Race-conscious parenting, on the other hand, can help children to be self-confident and proud of their identity.

20. "Some people say there is too much talk about race and racism in the United States. I say there is not enough. The twenty-year history I recounted in the prologue and the many examples throughout the preceding chapters highlight the pervasiveness of our problem. We need to continually break the silence about racism whenever we can." (Chapter 10, Page 331)

The culture of silence about racism is problematic, but there is no quick or easy way to fix it. Ideologies, such as the color-blind ideology which encourages silence, are deeply rooted and that makes it difficult to change them overnight. We as individuals are capable of challenging this ideology by speaking out against racism, but Tatum emphasizes that this dialogue needs to happen again and again.

21. "This woman was correct in her observation that most of the people of color in that classroom were more fluent in the discourse of racism and more aware of its personal impact on their lives than perhaps she was. But she was wrong that their participation was easy. They

were also afraid." (Chapter 10, Page 334)

Here, Tatum discusses a White woman's comments that she felt the students of color in her class had an easier time talking about racism. White people are often afraid of talking about racism, but they may not recognize that people of color are afraid too. Breaking the silence is difficult, but necessary, for everyone. White people are often afraid that they will say the wrong thing and people of color are often afraid that no one will listen to them, but everyone needs to overcome their fears.

22. "'What if I make a mistake?' you may be thinking. 'Racism is a volatile issue, and I don't want to say or do the wrong thing.' In almost forty years of teaching and leading workshops about racism, I have made many mistakes. I have found that a sincere apology and a genuine desire to learn from one's mistakes are usually rewarded with forgiveness. If we wait for perfection, we will never break the silence. The cycle of racism will continue uninterrupted." (Chapter 10, Page 341)

Pushing past one's fears is easier said than done. To encourage readers who are still afraid of making mistakes, Tatum indicates that she makes mistakes too, even as a leading expert on racism with decades of experience. Saying nothing at all is worse than accidentally saying the wrong thing.

23. "We must begin to speak, knowing that words alone are insufficient. But I have seen that meaningful dialogue can lead to effective action. Change is possible." (Chapter 10, Page 342)

Tatum's goal in this book is to help readers break the

silence about racism, but she acknowledges that simply talking about racism is not going to fix everything. Although dialogue in and of itself is not enough, it is an important starting point that can lead to more action. She repeatedly emphasizes her hope for a better future—if readers can be similarly inspired that they can produce change, then they too will speak up and take action.

24. "Can new cross-racial friendships change the racial climate of a city or the structural racism that is baked into its historical foundation and the map of its neighborhoods? There's no guarantee that it will, but it could. Institutional policies and practices are created and carried out by individuals, and when those individuals have homogeneous social networks, they too often lack empathy for those whose lives are outside their own frame of reference." (Epilogue, Page 346)

It may feel like having dialogues with friends, family, and acquaintances is not enough, but Tatum emphasizes that small changes can lead to big changes. Here, she discusses how the Atlanta Friendship Initiative has the power to foster greater empathy across social boundaries. Although people tend to think in "us versus them" terms, opening up a person's social network can expand who they consider to be "us."

25. "It has been said that to teach is to touch the future. Helping students to see the past more clearly, to understand and communicate with others more fully in the present, and to imagine the future more justly is to transform the world." (Epilogue, Page 358)

Throughout the book, Tatum has paid particular attention to the role that educational institutions and educators have played in both continuing and interrupting the cycle of racism. Tatum encourages educators to do the latter. They can teach the histories of marginalized groups that are often omitted from school curricula, they can teach students how to listen to one another, and they can inspire them to work toward a better future.

ESSAY TOPICS

1. Using the insights you have gained from this book, write about your own racial and/or ethnic identity development. Did you have any experiences that forced you to confront racism? Did you internalize negative messages about your own group and/or other groups? Did you ever seek support from same-group peers? Have you found a positive sense of racial/ethnic identity?

2. In Chapter 10, Tatum recommends that readers speak up about racism within their own sphere of influence. What is your sphere of influence? How can you break the silence about racism in your sphere? In the past, were there any incidents where you stayed silent instead of speaking up? If so, what could you have said?

3. Why do we need both intraracial and cross-racial dialogue about race and racism? What is the value of each?

4. What are the costs of racism for people of color? What are the costs for White people? What can we gain by speaking out against racism?

5. Compare and contrast the identity development process for Black people, other people of color, and White people. What similarities and differences are there in Cross', Helms', and Phinney's models? How does the identity development of multiracial individuals compare to that of monoracial people?

6. When discussing the identity development of each racial and ethnic group, Tatum incorporates a number of narratives in which members of these groups

describe their experiences in their own words. Looking at these narratives, what parallels and differences do you notice?

7. Think about the question posed in the title of the book. Why do people ask that question? What kinds of assumptions underlie it? Why did Tatum choose that to be the title?

8. Throughout the book, Tatum pays particular attention to the role of schools and educators. What role do they play in maintaining racism? What role can they play in interrupting racism? Why does Tatum focus so much on education as a site of ideological contention?

9. In response to a White woman who said she was "fighting for" people of color, Tatum says she recommended the woman "fight for herself, not for people of color" (332). What does Tatum mean by this? What does it mean to be an effective ally?

10. Tatum emphasizes throughout the book that we need "meaningful, productive dialogue" about racism (331). What makes dialogue meaningful and productive? What are some examples of dialogue that is not productive?

Made in the USA
Middletown, DE
23 December 2020